The International Taste Foodie

Travel and Food

Linda Lucia Swinney

The International Taste Foodie
TRAVEL AND FOOD

iUniverse books may be ordered through booksellers or by contacting:

iUniverse
1663 Liberty Drive
Bloomington, IN 47403
www.iuniverse.com
844-349-9409

Because of the dynamic nature of the Internet, any web addresses or links contained in this book may have changed since publication and may no longer be valid. The views expressed in this work are solely those of the author and do not necessarily reflect the views of the publisher, and the publisher hereby disclaims any responsibility for them.

Any people depicted in stock imagery provided by Getty Images are models, and such images are being used for illustrative purposes only.
Certain stock imagery © Getty Images.

ISBN: 978-1-6632-2188-9 (sc)
ISBN: 978-1-6632-2189-6 (e)

Library of Congress Control Number: 2021908466

Print information available on the last page.

iUniverse rev. date: 04/23/2021

Contents

Amazing Sirloin Steak & Herbs

Cook time: 20-25 mins Prep time: 10 mins Servings: 4

Ingredients: 4 6- 8 oz of sirloin steak, 4 oz of butter chopped 4 teaspoons of parsley 4 teaspoons of rosemary, thyme, and marjoram herbs. Small bowl putting in the bowl 4 teaspoons of olive oil. ½ cut onion finely chopped, 1 to 2 cups of dehydrated mushrooms, one and a half teaspoon of salt and pepper, 1 cup of red wine, 1 cup of beef stock warm up on medium to hot temperature, 2 cloves garlic peeled and finely chopped.

Directions: Melt the butter with oil and a skillet over medium heat. Add the onions and garlic cooking until softened. Add the thyme, mushrooms and sautee until warmed thoroughly. Add red wine and beef stock, bring to a boil. Reduce the heat, simmering until liquid reduces and thickens.

Steaks: Use cast iron skillet or griddle. Rub the steaks on both sides with oil, seasoned salt and pepper . Cook steaks in the pan and sear for 4 to 5 minutes per side until they're cooked to your desired doneness. Remove the steaks out of the pan and place on a plate for 5 minutes. Place each steak on its own plate and spoon the mushroom sauce over the top of the Steaks. Sprinkle on top the other herbs marjoram and rosemary. Lastly, topped with parsley and put some steak sauce on the a plate, and served with one of your favorite vegetables and salad. Eat and Enjoy!

Stuffed Green Peppers

Cook time: 2 hrs. Prep time: 20 mins Servings:4

Ingredients: 4 medium green bell peppers, remove tops and seeds and clean, 2 tablespoons of olive oil, 1 large chopped finely onion. 4 teaspoons of Worcestershire sauce, 2 large eggs, lightly beaten, 1 ½ cups shredded cheese of your choice; Preferably I had used mozzarella cheese as my choice with this particular meal but you may choose your choice of cheese. 1 cup of fresh chopped parsley. 2 cups of rice. 2 medium-sized tomatoes finely chopped, season to your liking as mild to hot herbs. 2 tablespoons of chopped fresh garlic. 1 pound of ground beef. Kostner salt sprinkle desired for your taste .

Directions: Preheat the oven to 350° degrees Fahrenheit. Add 2 in of water to the large pot fitted with the steamer insert, and bring to a high simmer. Arrange the peppers in the steamer, cover the pot and cook, rotating the peppers as needed, until they are very tender and pliable, about 25 minutes remove the peppers with the spoon, drain upside down on paper towels.

Combine pinch of salt, onions, oil all in a skillet over medium heat and cook stirring until the onions are soft for 8 minutes. Increase heat to medium to high. Add the beef, a few grinds of pepper, garlic, salt can be measured in a teaspoon.

1 teaspoon of salt. If I need to modify the quantity according to desired of the taste, then it can be adjusted. Cook all these ingredients together stirring and breaking the beef up until lightly brown can be cooked in 5 minutes. Then add the tomatoes, bringing to a simmer. Remove from heat. Let cool in the skillet for at least 10 minutes. Transfer to a large bowl, add in the rice, parsley, one cup of mozzarella cheese, or chosen desire cheese of your choice, eggs, and Worcestershire sauce and mixed to combine all together. Stand the peppers up and baking dish. I flattened the bottoms of my Peppers without cutting through the pepper itself. Fill and pack the peppers with the meat rice mixture, top with the rest of the cup of mozzarella cheese. Add just enough water to the pan to cover the bottom to help steam peppers. Cover with foil but not tightly cover. And bake until peppers are tender and filling heated through. In 30 minutes remove the foil and continue to bake for 10 more minutes. Afterwards cool down five to seven minutes, serve and eat!

Seafood Salmon Crumb Lemon Herb

Cook time:30 mins Prep time: 10 mins Servings:4

Ingredients: One salmon fillet, 1 ¼ lb. ⅓ teaspoon thyme leaves dried preferably, lemon thyme is similar to the English thyme. I used the lemon thyme,2 tablespoons of onion powder, 2 teaspoons of grated lemon peel, ¼ cup fresh white breadcrumbs wanted to slices depending on how crunchy you desire the salmon to taste, ¼ teaspoon of salt, 2 tablespoons of real butter melted, ¼ teaspoon cup parmesan cheese grated or ungrated.

Directions: Heat oven to 375° degrees Fahrenheit, spray baking pan with cooking spray for the base of the pan mildly spreading it at the bottom surface of the baking pan. Rinse the salmon and pat dry. Place Salmon skin side down in pan, brush salmon with 1 tbsp of butter, lightly sprinkled with salt over salmon. Mix in a small bowl bread crumbs, lemon peel, onions, cheese and thyme. Then stir and the remaining 1 tablespoon of butter. Press breadcrumb mixture evenly on the salmon. When baking keep uncovered for 10 to 20 minutes. Better to serve immediately after it's cooked nice and hot and fresh and all of the flavors that you added in will be actually up to the taste buds because it's fresh out of the oven. Side dish vegetables like broccoli, rice or any desired side of food that you decide to add as a side to the plate with your salmon. Serve and Eat!

Snow frosty mash potatoes meatloaf

Cook time: 1 hr Prep time: 30 mins Servings: 8

Ingredients 1 cup of milk,¼ cup of melted butter, 3 cups of mashed potatoes. I use the Idaho if I do not have the regular whole potatoes which normally that's what I prefer to use. You may use boxed potato flakes all natural 100 percent potatoes preferably Idaho potatoes. ¼ cup of brown sugar, 1 ½ cup of ketchup, 3 large beaten eggs, ¼ cup of fresh parsley,½ teaspoon of pepper, 1 teaspoon of salt. 2 lbs of ground beef, 1 cup of milk, 4 slices of bread.

Directions: Preheat oven at 350° degrees Fahrenheit. Put the bread slices in the mixing bowl and pour the milk over them and let the bread soak in the milk until it is fully absorb. Add ground beef, salt, black pepper and parsley to Bowl, mix up, add eggs, and mix again.

Shape the meat loaf inside the meatloaf pan. I used my meatloaf pan that has the inserted strainer to drip the grease from the meat which is perfect to use making meatloaf. Use a rack on the cooking pan of the pan that you plan on using for the meatloaf if you do not have a meatloaf pan. It functions the same as a meatloaf pan dropping with a regular baking pan, and a rack sitting on top of the baking pan. Then place the meatloaf on top of the rack. The grease will roll off at the bottom of the pan and the meatloaf is up above on the rack to where it is cooking evenly with the heat around it. Spread the ketchup brown sugar into a mixing bowl and stir it up and pour over the top of the meatloaf and spread it over the sides with a spatula. Bake you're meatloaf for 1 hour. Every oven cooks at different variations depending on the brand of the oven. So knowing the Dynamics of your oven is important. After the meatloaf is cooked for one hour take it out of the oven, and you let it sit for 5 to 7 minutes. increase the oven temperature to 450° degrees and cool meatloaf for 10 minutes then Frost the top and sides all the way around with the warm mashed potatoes with a brush add a spatula also with melted butter return to the oven and bake until potatoes or brown on the edges about 10 to 15 minutes. Then remove from the oven let it cool for a good 5 minute slice and serve. Eat!

Instant Barbeque Baby Back Ribs

Cook time: 25 mins Prep time: 10 mins Servings 4-6

Ingredients: 1 rack of baby back ribs or spare ribs remember spare ribs are thicker and they'll take longer to cook. 1 ½ pounds of spare ribs or baby back ribs. 1 cup of water, 3 tablespoons of apple cider vinegar, ½ teaspoons of liquid smoke, ¼ cup of homemade barbecue sauce or chosen sauces of your selection such as Baby Ray's barbecue sauce or any type of organic BBQ sauces or your homemade barbecue sauces whichever is of your desire. Or the rub seasonings to rub onto the ribs thoroughly. For the ribs is very important to add with the barbecue sauce the reasons are to soak in the flavors deeper and much more flavor of all. 2 tablespoons of brown sugar, 1 tablespoon of paprika, 1 teaspoon of chili powder, ¼ teaspoon of cayenne pepper, 1teaspoon of pepper, 1 teaspoon of salt, 1 teaspoon of garlic powder and 1 teaspoon of onion powder.

Instructions: Rinse the ribs and Pat them dry. If your ribs still have the thin shiny membrane on the back remove it, wiggle a dull knife between the membrane and the ribs in a small bowl, scared together the brown sugar, paprika, black pepper, salt, chili powder, garlic powder, onion powder and the cayenne pepper.

Rub it all over the ribs coating all the sides of the ribs. Cook time for the baby back ribs is 25 minutes on high pressure, heat plus 5 minutes natural release, spare ribs are tougher and they take longer to cook up to 35 minutes.

Cook on high pressure plus the natural release itself is going to cause it to cook instantly because it's locking in all the flavors in the heat altogether instantly. Don't vent the spare ribs immediately. The tougher meat ribs needs full natural release to become tender. Broil is a bonus task after the ribs are completed cooking its cycle. Brush the ribs with BBQ sauce and placed under the broiler for a few minutes. Lightly broil crisp on the top and the sauce becomes extra sweet and thick!

Directions continued here on the instant pot ribs. If you're cooking two packs of racks you can actually cook them together by using a trick and overlap them inside one another if needed and it should not change much of the cooking time. Sauce it up choose your favorite top sauce for the ribs one of my favorites is Sweet Baby Ray's BBQ sauce. Seems to seal the deal for the taste buds! Side dish can add a sense of Flair to your barbecue ribs such as a vegetable, baked potato, or seasoned french fries. Make sure you use a Dry Rub on the ribs also remove the membranes of the ribs. To soak in the flavors much better remove the membrane that extra room will be able to filter the seasonings better and give it more flavor. Towards the end of the ribs cook time, place a rack in the upper part of your oven and set the cooking function broil, remove ribs from crock pot, and place ribs on a baking sheet with aluminum foil. Transferred to cook ribs from the pot to the baking sheet pan on the aluminum foil and then brush ribs liberally with barbecue sauce. Broil for 10 minutes, remove from oven, cool 5-7 minutes and serve, Bon Appetit!

Mama Mia~ Lucia's Italian Sausage and Pasta

Cook time: 50 mins Prep time: 30mins Servings:6

Ingredients: 1 tbsp of butter, 1 cup of progresso bread crumbs, ½ cup of tablespoon of olive oil, 1 pound of mild Italian sausage, one cup of diced onions,one cup of diced red bell peppers, one cup of diced green peppers,2 tablespoons of Italian seasonings, 12 oz of penne pasta, bowtie pasta or any selected choice of pasta, 1 cup of fresh diced tomatoes, one carton of chicken broth, ½ cup of Italian blended cheese.

Directions: In an 8-inch Skillet, melt butter over low heat, up to 5 minutes. Stir until Brown put into the bowl set to the side. In a dutch oven pot, heat oil over medium heat and place the sausage inside the pan and cook up to 8 minutes. Stirring occasionally until no more pink color is shown,place sausages on a plate and set it to the side. Add onions, bell peppers red- green, Italian seasonings, salt, oil and drippings in the pan, cook over medium heat minutes until softened and starting to Brown. Stirring broth and tomatoes in pan to heat. Stir-In pasta return to Boiling, reduce heat to simmer uncovered 15 to 20 minutes. Stirring occasionally sauce is thickening, stir sausage until limp. Remove from heat and top with Italian Blended cheese and parsley. Ready to eat!

Spanish Sherry Chicken Quarter Legs

Cook time: 45mins

Prep time:10 to 15 mins Servings: 8

Ingredients: 4 chicken leg quarters to fresh thyme, 1 Orange, 2 to 3 whole tomatoes finely diced, 2 ½ oz of Sherry cooking wine,1 ½ cups of chopped onion, salt and pepper dispersing pinches to your desired taste desired.

Instructions preheat oven to 350° degrees Fahrenheit on the stove heat Skillet to the medium to high heat. Season chicken legs with salt and pepper; Stir the chicken on both sides until the skin is golden in color remove from the pan and set aside. Add onion to the pan with the Sherry cooking wine. Deglaze the pan and sautee the onions in the liquid until it evaporates. Next add tomatoes, orange zest and herb's stir and combine, and return the chicken to the pan. Then transfer to the oven and bake for 45 minutes. Check the chicken legs with a fork to make sure it is fully cooked. Once it is fully cooked, then you can remove the chicken from the cooking pan and onto a serving platter plate, allowing it to cool down for 5 to 10 minutes. And then ready to serve eat!

Italian Spaghetti Sauce

Cook time: 4 hrs Prep time:20 mins

Servings: 8

Ingredients: 1 ½ pounds of Lean ground beef, medium yellow onion diced up finely cut, ½ cup 4 cloves garlic finely minced, 2 28 Oz can of crushed Roma tomatoes, Contadina brand is one of the best that I use. ¼ cup of chopped fresh basil. 2 tblspns of chopped fresh parsley. 1 teaspoon of Rosemary herb, ¾ teaspoon of dried fine, ½ teaspoon of dried oregano herb, ½ teaspoon of dried marjoram, ½ teaspoon of dried sage, ½ bay leaves, ½ teaspoon of salt to your desired taste, ¼ teaspoon of freshly ground black pepper, ½ to 1 cup of beef broth to thin sauce as desired. Add freshly find grated Parmesan and Romano cheese.

Instructions: In a large sauce pot, add one tablespoon of olive oil over low heat. Crumble ground beef into pot stir it occasionally. Breaking up the beef as you stir it until cooked thoroughly. Drain the ground beef, Place ground beef and a food processor until finally grounded about 15 seconds and set aside. Then sauteed the onions over medium-high heat until golden color or garlic during the last minute of the sauteing. Removed from the heat reducing splattering and stir cans of crushed Roma tomatoes remaining 3 tablespoons of extra-virgin olive oil, basil, parsley, rosemary, thyme, oregano,marjoram,sage, bay leaves, salt, pepper and browned beef; Return pot to low heat and simmer uncovered 4 hours stirring occasionally, add beef broth to sauce too thin sauce if desired. If not, skip adding in any broth. Like thick spaghetti sauce no adding broth. Remove the bay leaves and serve sauce warm over pasta. Add grated cheeses for extra taste- punch to the spaghetti dinner and a few fresh parsleys for added look in appearance to the pasta dish. Now ready to serve, Mangia!

Italian Lasagna Rollups

Cook time: 1 hr Prep time: 20 mins Servings: 6

Ingredients: 12 lasagna cooked noodles for 2 minutes till it soft but not overly soft. ½ pound of lean ground beef. Italian sausage can be used instead of beef. ½ a cup of grated Parmesan cheese. 2 cups of ricotta cheese. Salt, pepper and any Italian herbs to your desire. 1 tablespoon of Italian seasoning, or more to your taste. 13 oz of spaghetti sauce or marinara sauce. ½ teaspoon of garlic powder. ½ teaspoon of onion powder. 1 teaspoon of Basil.

Note: Even though boiled 12 lasagna noodles, I did this because I put two lasagna noodles together rather than one lasagna noodle when I roll the lasagna together this will reinforce the noodles while rolling them and making the roles a little thicker.

Method: Brown the beef meat with the onion powder or whole onion cut up over the medium heat. Drain grease and then add the garlic and cook extra 1 to 2 minutes. Add spaghetti sauce and any Italian Seasonings let it simmer for 12 to 15 minutes. Add salt and pepper added in till the desired taste; then add the ricotta cheese. Preheat oven to 350° degrees Fahrenheit, pour some sauce on the bottom of the casserole dish. For my rolls I use a cookie sheet. Take two double strips of lasagna noodles place one lasagna noodle on top of another noodle. There will be making 6 lasagna rolls, thick and not thin rolls. Spread the ricotta cheese on the top of the noodles spreading the cheese thoroughly on the entire top and length. Add ¼ cup of meat sauce down the middle of the noodles then proceeded to roll the lasagna and a roll form shape. Placed in a casserole dish. Any extra sauce put it on the top and around the sides of the pan. Sprinkle mozzarella cheese on top. Cover with boil and bake in a preheated oven for 25 minutes. Remove boil and bake an additional 10 to 20 minutes, or until golden color. Allowed to set for 5 minutes to cool before serving it. Top with fresh or dried basil, if desired.Ready to Eat.

Oma's German Rouladen

Recipe: Cook time: 1hr 30 minutes Prep time: 40 minutes Servings: 8

Ingredients ⅓ cup of flour, 2 ½ cups of beef broth, 2 tablespoons of olive oil toothpicks salt and pepper to you desired taste, ¼ cup of Dijon mustard or German brand mustard like Inglehoffer brand. Three whole dill pickles cut in thin slices, three carrots cut them in thin slices, one onion large, cut thin slices, 8 slices of bacon, ⅔ pounds of topside steak, (round roast) cut in slices. ½ cup of clean water with fresh chopped parsley.

Directions: Take a basting brush and spread the German or Dijon mustard on the slices of steak, lightly sprinkled pinches of salt and pepper place a strip of bacon and some onions, carrots, pickles, then began rolling up the steak in a (roll shape) and secure with toothpick. Next use a skillet pan, putting the beef in the skillet to Brown and the olive oil till pink in color. Drain it, adding in beef broth. Raise temperature to high as it boils then decrease the Heat; Allow simmer for 1 hour and 30 minutes minutes or until the meat is tender. Take meat out of the skillet keeping it warm in a dish or bowl with a lid covering. This will help keep the heat in. Combine flour, stir in the beef broth bringing to a boil with consistent stirring till it is thick. Remove toothpicks. Lastly, return the beef to the gravy. Sprinkle with parsley if desired. Ready to serve and eat.

Italian Brushetta

Cook time: 20 mins Prep time: 15 mins Servings:12

Ingredients: 1 cup of shredded mozzarella or Pearl mozzarella cheese that's in a whole and cut up in Pearl sizes, garlic cloves smashed fine, 1 ½ tbsp of Extra Virgin Olive virgin oil, 1 French baguette loaf, cut in a ½ inch sizes, 2 tablespoons of Rosemary herbs or you can use other herbs such as thyme or basil herbs, 1 cup of cherry tomatoes wash them thoroughly clean, ¼ teaspoon of salt in ¼ teaspoon of pepper, a ½ a tablespoon of balsamic vinegar.

Directions: preheat oven to 300 ° degrees Fahrenheit. Put tomatoes on a baking pan and pour the extra virgin olive oil and balsamic vinegar over the top of the tomatoes, sprinkle a pinch of salt and pepper. Roast for 20 minutes until the tomatoes are piping hot in sight seeing that WOW! Expression from the popping cherry tomatoes. Use a griddle pan or a regular pan, heat till it's hot, brush the sides of the french baguette bread on both sides a bit with extra virgin olive oil. Toasting each side of the bread on the pan until the edges are golden brown. Rubbing each toasted bread with garlic. Add three of the tomatoes to a slice of toast baguette adding a couple of slices of mozzarella cheese and add Rosemary herbs or your choice of Herb's on top of the mozzarella cheese of the bruschetta. Lastly finish pinching salt and pepper on the top giving added flavor to the bruschetta. Can be eaten cold or warm. Ready to eat.

Beef Bourguignon

Cook time: 1 hr Prep time: 45 mins

Servings:6

Recipe: Cauliflower rice or a few other side entres can be served with Brisket or round steak. Dry red wine, Pinot Noir.

Ingredients: 1 3 pound brisket, 1 tablespoon of parsley finely chopped, 1ounce of porcini mushroom washed well and cut in quarters. 2 tbsp of butter unsalted, 1 tbsp of olive oil, 3 cups of Pinot Noir wine dry red wine, excellent for this dish. Start the water boiling. 2 cups of beef stock, 2 tbsp of all purpose flour, 1 tbsp of tomato paste, 1 fresh bay leaf, ½ tspn of chopped basil, 5 carrots, peeled and cleaned and chopped, 4 to 5 garlic cloves chopped, 1 cup of pearl White onions, 1 large yellow onion cut in slices, salt and pepper to taste, 4 slices of bacon.

Instructions: Preheat oven to 350° degrees Fahrenheit, cut the beef and 2 inches thick cubes, season with salt and pepper. Heat and in Dutch oven over medium heat going to do some sauteing the bacon till it's crispy. Take the bacon out of the pan then set aside save the Fat from the pan turn the temperature up to hot high Sear the beef and in the hot fat. Searing both sides til browned. After 9 minutes, remove beef and put it on the plate with the bacon. All meat must go through the same steps to all be is seared. Afterwards, turn heat down to medium, add carrots, sliced onions and pearl white onions to the pan. Onions being sauteed until lightly brown and tender enough for 12 minutes. Then add bay leaf, basil, tarragon, garlic to sauteed, For 20 seconds. Add the tomato paste, sautee for 20 seconds. Sprinkle flour, and steer and cook for 2 minutes. Steer and beef stock. Add Pinot Noir wine helps the flowers that can up the sauce. Add in the bacon and the beets simmering liquid for a few minutes. Cover and transfer pot to the oven. Meat cook still tender up to 1 hour and 45 minutes. Then prep mushrooms and heat up a large Skillet pan over low heat. Adding olive oil, butter, wait till the bubbling and then add the mushrooms. Saute the mushrooms until brown and tender. Afterwards sprinkle ¼ teaspoon salt for 2 minutes, monitoring the meat and when done cooking, transfer meat to the vegetables to large bowl. The sauce should be simmering over a low heat. That rises to surface use the spoon to take off the excess fat. Sauce being reduced till it can coat the back and of the spoon. Test the labor and seasoned more with salt and pepper if needed. Meat is then returned to vegetables, mushrooms stirring until warm and put chopped parsley as the garnish ready to serve and Eat!

Asian Peanut Sauce

Cook time: 5 mins Prep time: 5 mins

Servings:4

Ingredients: ½ cup of peanut butter, 2 tbsp of soy sauce, 1 tbsp of white sugar, 2 drops of hot pepper sauce. 1 clove of garlic(minced equals ½ tspn of minced garlic). ½ tspn giner, ½ cup of water.

Directions: Mix all ingredients together in a small mixing bowl then add peanut butter, soy sauce, hot pepper sauce, sugar, minced clove garlic, ginger, and mix all together thoroughly. Adding water a little at a time.

Note: Taste the peanut sauce and if it needs an ingredient adjustment of any kind, then add what ingredient(s)may be lacking, quantity wise. Your taste buds pallet will signal to you what may be lacking ingredients wise. Everyone's taste buds are different.

Note: Texture of peanut sauce is better when smooth and creamy, pourable. Peanut sauce is good tasting over tofu,veggies, meets in dippables. Peanuts sauce is ready to serve to Eat.

Swedish Meatballs

Cook time: 30 mins Prep time:20 mins

Servings:6-8

Ingredients: ⅓ cup of sour cream, 3 cups of beef stock, ¼ cup of all-purpose flour, 3 tbsp of unsalted butter, 1 tbsp of olive oil, salt and black pepper desires, ¼ tspn ground nutmeg, ¼ tspn of ground allspice, 2 tbsp of fresh parsley, to green onions finely sliced, 2 large egg yolks, ⅓ cup of Panko bread crumbs, ¾ lbs of ground pork, ¾ lbs of ground beef, 8 oz of noodles preferably egg noodles or other pasta noodles of your choice.

Directions: Take one large pot of boiling, salted water cook pasta according to package. Drain very well. In a large bowl, combine ground pork, beef, Panko bread crumbs, egg yolks, green onions, parsley, allspice and nutmeg seasonings, 1 teaspoon; of salt and 1 teaspoon of pepper; Using a spoon, clean until well combined. Roll the mixture into 1 -¼ inch Meatballs forming about 24 meatballs. Heat olive oil in a large Skillet over medium to high heat. Add meatballs, in batches and cook until all sides are brown, about 2 to 3 minutes. Then transfer to a paper towel- lined plate: Set aside.

Swedish meatball sauce ingredients: Quarter cup of butter over medium heat, half a cup of flour with in with the butter to form a paste picking up gravy. Quarter of a cup of Worcestershire sauce, 4 cups of beef broth, "A Roux" will cause the beef stock to thicken and come to a boil. ½ teaspoon of nutmeg, ½ teaspoon of allspice turn the sauce to low heat. ¾ cups a sour cream and whisk it in till it›s smooth. Add salt and pepper to desired taste. Keep gravy over warm Heat. Add butter to the noodles so they do not stick together. Garnish the dish with fresh parsley. Serve and eat!

Limey British Shepherd's Pie

Cook time: 1 hr Prep time: 20 mins Servings: 6

Cooking equipment needed: Large pot,skillet will be used for layering the meat. Chopping board, knife, wooden spoon, and potatoes masher.

Meat layer shepherd's pie ingredients: 2 pounds of beef or lamb minced ½ tspn of marjoram, 1 tspn of Rosemary, 2 bay leaves, 2 tbsp of tomato puree, 2 tbsp of Worcestershire sauce, 2 cloves of garlic minced, 1 onion, finely diced, 2 sticks of celeries -cut diced, 2 carrot sticks cut diced, ½ a cup of red wine, 2 ½ cups of beef stock, extra virgin olive oil and salt and pepper add to your taste desires.

Mash layer: 4.4 lb of peeled potatoes cut diced, ½ cup of half-and-half, 4 tbsp of unsalted butter, ½ tspn of nutmeg, ½ a cup of grated Parmesan or the topping of the shepherd's pie, salt and pepper to your desired taste.

Directions: Heat skillet over medium heat, add meat breaking it up and using the spoon turning it in the skillet until it begins to brown, seasoned with salt and pepper. Continue cooking, until fully Brown and then pour into a baking dish. Then add more extra virgin olive oil as needed adding in carrots, celery & onion, cooking it until it softens and brown. Adding garlic, cook for 2 minutes longer, stir in tomato puree, deglaze with wine allowing to reduce heat for a few minutes. Add meat and stir combining all together.

Poor beef stock in Worcestershire sauce, add bay leaves, rosemary, marjoram, salt and pepper to your desired taste. Simmer til thickened.

Boil potatoes in salted water until they're tender. Test with a knife. Drain potatoes mash them add butter. Remove any lumps. Stir in Cream half-and-half and seasoned with salt, pepper and nutmeg.

Pour meat into a baking dish, topping with mashed potatoes. Top shepherd's pie with Parmesan cheese and put the baking dish in the oven at 380° degrees Fahrenheit for 20 minutes or until golden colored brown on top.

Take out the baking dish from the oven and allow to sit and cool a few minutes. Ready to eat!

Printed in the United States
by Baker & Taylor Publisher Services